# New financial order

## order

N.F.O.

Brandon McYntire

ISBN 978-93-5667-278-9
© Brandon McYntire 2023
Published in India 2023 by Pencil

**Contributors:**
Co-Author: Brandon McYntire

*A brand of*
One Point Six Technologies Pvt. Ltd.
123, Building J2, Shram Seva Premises,
Wadala Truck Terminal, Wadala (E)
Mumbai 400037, Maharashtra, INDIA
**E** connect@thepencilapp.com
**W** www.thepencilapp.com

*All rights reserved worldwide*

No part of this publication may be reproduced, stored in or introduced into a retrieval system, or transmitted, in any form, or by any means (electronic, mechanical, photocopying, recording or otherwise), without the prior written permission of the Publisher. Any person who commits an unauthorized act in relation to this publication can be liable to criminal prosecution and civil claims for damages.

DISCLAIMER: *The opinions expressed in this book are those of the authors and do not purport to reflect the views of the Publisher.*

# Author biography

My ancestors came to Czechoslovakia from the US specifically from Baltimore. My grandmother Elizabth Grace McIntyre died in our town Michalovce, Czechoslovakia. I gave a pseudonym after her - McYntire.I changed my last name because - McYntire liked it more literaryly. I'm 41 years old. So it's the real name of my American ancestors. I graduated from a technical university, but I never enjoyed it and I started writing in school. in elementary school I started writing a short story - Island 2289. After many years - over 20 years, I rediscovered it among old papers and finished it two years ago. I am divorced and I have two daughters from first marriage. My relationship to writing culminated in my writing of mysterious and mysterious stories. Gradually, I started to translate some of them (the best ones) into English and registered with KDP. My writing journey to the whole English-speaking world has begun. I believe you will like my work and I will try to write many books.

He graduated as the last school in the postgraduate TIS extension in the town of Michalovce in Slovakia in the European Union.
He was already prone to writing in elementary school, despite the fact that he described himself as an average to weak student. The short story ISLAND 2289 is one of

those that he began writing in his seventh grade in elementary school. After finding about ten pages of this short story among the old papers, he decided to finish this interesting story. He completed it this year (2016) and was subsequently published as a short story ..

The first book, ABOUT THE STARS (2015), raised questions and disillusionment for readers. The author himself never commented publicly on whether it was a real life story or fiction. This book and the author himself were accompanied by problems from the very beginning of the book to its withdrawal from circulation.

In r. In 2017, all works in the second edition went back on sale.

The author is a sympathizer of esoterics, science and pseudoscience. He wrote the short story IN THE CITY OF LOIST on the basis of dreams. He allegedly writes down dreams and, after a long time, looks for connections in them.

This is an unimaginable and impossible matter for the average reader. It is supposedly just a basic technique for looking into other spheres - visions of the future. It is impossible to disregard the reality that the author is generally oriented in this area. At the expense of it, evil tongues are constantly creating new alternatives around him. The author rejects all these attacks.

As he put it in one interview, "I've always been interested in things between heaven and earth, but not occultism!"

The author has written to date, i. February 20222, a total of 34 Slovak books and many of them were translated into other languages.

English, French, Chinese, Russian, Hebrew, German and other languages. He also has audiobooks on his account.

His books are sold all over the world and he has many readers in Israel and Taiwan. The English versions of his books are sold mainly on platforms such as Amazon, Barnes and Noble, Googlay Play, Overdrive and thousands of online and physical libraries around the world.

# CONTENTS

# First meeting

The first meeting.

Neither during the time of King Charles I the Great, nor for many centuries after that, our predecessors in Europe understood this. The effort to change and order some zealots was useless. They did not understand the essence of chaos. I am not surprised, at that time of the beginning of great chaos, and in fact until recently, people could not look at it from a perspective with the support of a more extensive study. Efforts to improve the situation were without a clear result, as their ideas and knowledge were insufficient. This was confirmed by the fact that they did not achieve their goals. One thing is certain. Kings, dictators, presidents and heads of government have never achieved an order that would last. Maybe some of them managed to do something, but only for a limited time: from - to. A then everything started to fall apart again. Chaos ensued, in which no one, not even a representative of the monarchy or state power, and certainly not simple people, could understand. We can compare it to the scenario of a theater play, but from which we can learn a lot. The monarchy was often very selfish and in essence could be compared, especially in its initial phase, to the dictatorship of state power. It couldn't go on like this forever. At the same time, chaos spread with attempts at overall order and a clearer social arrangement. Monarchs and state officials introduced laws and social rules that were supposed to prevent chaos. Maybe some were quite successful, but not for long. Mostly it was just their delusions that they had everything under control. But it didn't happen. All aspects of disruption and they strengthened the chaos even more. At the same time, they behaved so superficially that they did not even notice that everything is actually managed by subtle government minions who should support them and not mistrust them. Dictatorships that have emerged in Europe since the time of Napoleon have shown an effort to order some kind of society by force. The wars they waged were brutal, causing millions of innocent victims, spreading suffering, disease and misery. Nazism, Communism and various other isms are just ideologies that are also doomed at their very end. The junkyard of political establishments shows us the inevitable fall of any tyranny at the end of any long period. It's all vanity. It has no perspective when the action of chaos is constantly present. What's more, it seems to be gaining strength as a result of these alternating political establishments. From this point of view, it is really debatable in which period the chaos intensified the most. During the monarchy? In the period of the bourgeois republic? During the dictatorship? In the era of capitalism? In the era of democracy? We can only argue about the endless thesis of consequences leading to the decline of any social establishment. Violation of normality, disrespect of basic values in people's lives, turning away from truth, justice, love for one's neighbor - they only increase human madness. It is present at every step of our life, our being. A mistake that may have happened at the very beginning of civilization. We stepped in the wrong direction. We can already see it today. We understood that it was driving humanity to its doom. In those days it was impossible to see more clearly. However, today we have statistics and many other methods available to provide us with an estimate and an accurate calculation.

Today has come the day when we can decide and commit to a fundamental step. All the while, the humanity of the world had it right in front of their eyes. We have to come to our senses now. We will seize the opportunity to fight against the global chaos and start building the pillars of a new life. Nothing will stop us from going on the right path. On the way to global peace and equality. It's about time. All it takes is a little and we will start a completely new era of humanity. We will lay the foundations of a new world and demolish systems operating on the old foundations of error, cruelty and greed. Nothing purposeful! There will be no place for profiteers and subversive elements. The strategy we create will thwart the hypocritical plans of any organization or association. It will not be possible to plan and organize things ahead on an old world platform. It will not be compatible with what we create anew. The world we've been striving for for centuries keeps eluding us. We have never come close to ideals, to our desires and ideas of a just society. Not even a third of what was in the plans of the wiser and fairer part of society.

This is the first meeting or our first meeting. I have called you to take action, because what is beginning to happen beyond our borders confirms once again that all efforts so far have been futile. Really enough! It is time to step in and reshape the global system as we have long intended and as we have planned for many years ahead. But we have to start as soon as possible. Already today. We don't have time because we are facing a global catastrophe! We will not resurrect later, we will not put together a civilization as such. We can't wait and let everything flow by itself. After all, we understand very well what that means. All of us gathered here must unite. Because if we don't make our best effort, we are doomed. If we do not do this, then in the coming millennia, only archaeologists, forensic anthropologists and other researchers will discover the remains, artifacts and debris of our civilization under the deposits of sand and earth. And that has happened many times in this world. Our quest now is to avert the downfall of our civilization. If we all want to survive, let's start today to build a new structure of society and fulfill the visions of a new world. The world of the merciful and just. A world without violence, wars, crime, misery and suffering. We will remove all the ills of society forever. We will create a world where no one is poor or homeless. Every citizen of this society will have access to whatever they need. Health services, food, housing, education and goods in shops at a low price. So that everyone can afford whatever they need and whatever they like. We will produce and sell everything that we can even imagine, so that no citizen suffers from shortages and that everyone's needs are met. There will be no need for meaningless state demands on citizens to obey the system. We will give everyone absolute freedom and a satisfied life in any part of the world. Protection of every person and their life.

Dear friends, this is the first meeting where I will present to you the basic points of the provisions of the new concept. At the second meeting, which we will call later, we will discuss the fair arrangement of state borders and their system, which will be much more effective than determining state borders. Well, today I called you for the first part. In it, I want to focus on removing the chaotic arrangement of the entire world and proposals for building solid pillars of the new future. Thank you for coming. Well, I want to warn you again to take note that this is a strictly secret meeting. All of you who are here have sworn, and you made a promise. Behind closed doors in front of the media and the outside world, we will discuss everything necessary according to the plan. Nothing we establish today will get past this metal door. The entire meeting room is arranged in such a way that neither eavesdropping nor localization from satellites is possible. Be that as it may, they are our devices, with the help of which we control everything. I already issued instructions last night to divert the interception satellites and deciphering voices. They are equipped with the most sophisticated computer technology. We have motion points in front of us to go through. At the end of this meeting, we must establish new rules and a new plan that we will immediately begin to apply at the highest levels of management organizations and government institutions. I have already sent a signal to the management of all the world's banks that an important change will soon occur. They will get new guidelines and a new plan that is essential for the banking industry. I hope that their representatives will be very vigilant and understand that what is presented to them is extremely important. After all, these responsible workers should already have a high level of financial understanding. Other interested organizations will also receive amended guidelines, with which they will gradually familiarize themselves, as pupils from the first year of primary school do. They will learn everything that involves the alphabetical arrangement of the new system. We will start creating it today. The consistent mechanism of our new society and world.

Dear friends, it is eight o'clock in the morning and today I have to make clear to you the appropriate changes that we will subsequently make through governments, organizations and banks. There are exactly ten of you and that is the number of votes needed to enact the presented concept and to start a new process. After this and subsequently, after our second meeting, you will be obliged to expand and apply this new concept within our company. First through the media, as always, and then you focus on the highest posts and chairs of politicians, which must be changed forever, but several of them must be removed forever. It is in your power because we have entrusted you. We put the power in your hands and it is now unlimited.

We don't have much time left to approve and start the process. Armed conflicts and wars have already broken out beyond the borders, in which both soldiers and many civilians die. There is still organized crime and various other crimes for profit.

The time has come to hit the right spots. To throw the devil into hell itself and never allow him to come to the surface of this Earth again. It can be done and we will do it. Because we actually unconsciously created and summoned the devil. And we will destroy him now. Once and for all. We will establish worldwide peace, equality and tranquility among nations. We know what we need to remove. And we will remove it forever. Because we created everything. What we have created for centuries, we will now simply remove. We are starting to build the pillars of a new social system, a new just world. Our task is to build and strengthen. Change and arrange. Delete old ones and create new ones. Our old house is falling apart on bad foundations and wrong estimates. Perhaps what has been until now was necessary for us to be shown the right model. A model of the new world. As someone said: New world. The golden age.

# Point one. Abolition of physical money.

Ladies and gentlemen, we are starting the first session. The first rally. The first topic of our meeting. A topic about money and its harmful impact on society.

A clear part of the disaster that has troubled and destroyed entire nations many times is represented by money. Physical money. There is a saying - money makes the world go round. But I would define it more precisely - money destroys the world. They destroy the lives of entire families as well individuals. Money guaranteed to cause disasters in society as such. Villains appeared straight from the depths of hell. They are responsible for the spread of crime in every area of life. A man could take a man's life even for the smallest amount of money or take cruel revenge if he felt wronged or if he did not get what he wanted from the other. Organized criminal groups emerged. Shop with by people. Prostitution. And ultimately the drug trade. The latter stands at the highest level of efforts to make a profit from all areas of immoral trading. All this was created and grew to monstrous proportions before our eyes. It was caused by the social system we created and set up incorrectly. Money from various sources of income was slipping through our fingers. Those that we could distribute among weaker social groups. We could use them to meet all the needs of the company. We have wrongly invested money, but also time, in elected heads of state - presidents, prime ministers, who ultimately failed and were defeated. We have shifted possibilities, investments and hopes to the wrong ideals. People couldn't deal with it and never will. Because they live in a world that won't allow them to. It is necessary to set up the new system in such a way that we will no longer be able to use the familiar reasoning - the human factor has failed. I don't mean any robot. But the system. No one will be able to change the system we set up. No one who will stand at the head of the state. No new elected president, prime minister, politician or banker. It will be a system on the platform of electronic order and prohibition. A new social system for man and society. Well, rather for the person himself, because the company will function relatively alone. It will no longer be threatened by scoundrels, criminals, gangs that seek to satisfy their own interests and whose goal is to make a profit. And not by the wars of other states, which would like to seize by force what does not belong to them, and that only from a position of strength and in favor of their own interests. So far, we have worked out in detail the first two points, which relate to what we need to implement. We will already create the following points and monitor the possibilities of their application after the emergence of a new political-economic system and after changes in our society.

Today I present to you the first point.

We will abolish paper, metal coins and other current forms of payment for good. We will turn them into numbers. Those numbers will be covered by the system and it will not be possible to send and give them for nothing. We will dispose of material money. We will melt down the metal coins and use them to make various other things. We will recycle the paper and also use it to make other paper things. Encoded numbers will be owned by banks and in the form of numbers they will be sent to people as payments for work and also make all other possible payments to payment cards. Perhaps rather for the chips that we apply to adults after reaching adulthood. We do not yet know what age we will determine in the new world for a citizen to reach adulthood. We assume that neither ATM nor other cards will make sense. We will cancel those as well, because they could create a potential threat to the citizen that he could become a victim of a robbery. In the new world, the citizen will not have to carry any wallet or plastic cards. This will prevent the initial risk of robbery and theft. The miniature microchip, which we apply under the skin on the left hand of an adult citizen, will work on the basis of absolutely flawless communication between the bank and all other authorities. It will contain identification data about the person of the citizen instead of the identity card. After all, we know very well how much fraud and crime has also become identity theft. Simply by stealing another person's identity card and misusing the information. Nor will ID cards of a physical nature be required. They would only harm things. We have reached the age of developed information technology and technology, which are introduced in all spheres of society 's life , when it is possible to manage everything necessary electronically from space. We have satellites that can even find a lost mouse in the desert. Nothing physical for payment or proof of identity is needed anymore. Finally, now we can create a society that we will manage, monitor, but ultimately we can also change, shape or eliminate something if it is in the interest of saving humanity.

Dear ones, I will now explain to you what will happen if we abolish physical money. Please listen carefully and watch this board which will show our statistical and political estimates. We recruited the best political scientists and financiers from all corners of the world to create, summarize and provide a final justification. They worked on this project continuously for a whole year, day after day. Their work and effort to create a new social and financial order was duly rewarded. After the introduction of the new system, we will give them various advantages and benefits and they will be part of the group of peacemakers. The peacemaker plaque will be placed in this country in the capital so that all citizens can see it. But I will explain that only in the second part at our big second meeting. So please concentrate, now I am going to tell you about what will happen after the abolition of physical money.

The second day after the abolition of physical money, there will be a change in the thinking of the entire financial world. Citizens will no longer have to carry a wallet or any plastic or other document. He will have a microchip implanted on his left wrist, which will be immediately activated that day and also eligible for financial transactions and payments. There will no longer be cash registers in stores for accepting physical money. Those in of the same denomination as the day before, will be converted into numbers that will contain the microchip in the left hand. Citizens will be able to buy common necessities on the first day and food the same as the day before. The only difference will be that he will put his left hand to the glass reading panel and that will be paid. The value of the purchase is deducted from the microchip v left hand.

The citizen will be part of the financial process. We will not move money and burden the entire system and ecosystem. We will send the numbers. As much as the citizen will have earned or admitted. The system will not be bypassed. The numbers will be of a special, electronic and banking nature. They will not be ordinary numbers that can be sent via e-mail or through some social media. These numbers will be exclusively owned by the banks. So we. We will treat the entire system on a new operating basis. We already believe that one financial center in each country will be enough for us. There would be no need for different banks and branches as it was until now. One bank with approximately five employees will be enough for the entire system of operation. We will lighten the administration and the banking system as a whole, we will reduce costs to ten percent compared to today's one hundred percent. We will have minimal costs and worries about the banking system. One state, one bank. The numbers will be exclusively in our hands. IT technology specialists are already at the end of creating this new system. They work continuously 24 hours a day. Now you have to think on new levels and completely forget the principles you know today. The numbers we will own will change the world for the better. It may seem unbelievable to you, but it will be so. We have already said - enough! It is high time to introduce a new financial order. We used the international abbreviation - NFO. IN English – New

Financial Order. Why is that so? I'll explain it to you right now. We thought that money, that is, physical money, was an essential part of the functioning of this world, but it was a mistake. A mistake that has no parallel and has caused so much war and suffering that it can no longer go on like this. That's why we accelerated the entire process of transferring from money to numbers. I will now give you simple examples to understand what we already knew during the existence of monarchies in Europe, but we had no available means to change it. Today we already have everything we need. Internet, computers, mobile phones, satellites and satellites in space. Now is the time to make this correction and create a new world.

# Example number 1. Street crime.

Dear friends, we live in a time when a citizen is able to deprive another citizen of even the minimum financial amount he has in his wallet. We are talking about street crime. So the basic motive and reason for this social negative phenomenon is the physical money of the attacked citizen. It's a simple equation. If the citizen did not have any money in his wallet, perhaps the robbery and crime would not have happened at all. Although the attacker does not even know at first whether the victim of the attack even has any money in his wallet, it is enough for him to carry out the robbery just to think. And there is already crime in the world. One does not have to be a psychologist to be able to perceive a clear connection. It's not complicated at all. Now, everyone, imagine how it would turn out if the attacker was aware that this citizen did not have any physical money with him. Because there wouldn't even be any physical money! Would he have a reason to ambush in the streets and rob? Not. It wouldn't make sense. And so, in this case, we actually eliminated the citizen's urge to raid and rob. They erased this crime from human society. He wouldn't exist. The system of the new financial order would not allow this type of crime to even arise. We spend an incredible amount of money to fight crime. We manage police departments and strive for the impossible. Eliminate the crime that physical money generated here by itself. It's an escape to nowhere. The police generally fight crime in the streets as well, but they never manage to destroy the source of this evil. It only comes into conflict with the resulting consequences of physical money. We are trying to fight against something that we have unwittingly supported so that it can arise and spread on a large scale. What follows from this simple example? Well, a completely simple equation. After the introduction of NFO and the abolition of physical money, we will forever eliminate one part of a negative phenomenon in society. Street crime focused on robbery will disappear!

# Example number 2. Major crime for profit.

Now imagine an ordinary drug dealer standing on any street corner in any city. He is just a distributor at the very end of the criminal chain. From citizen X, he receives material to sell and instructions on where to go and at what price to sell each item. That is, drugs to the final consumer. To the weak condemned to death because of their own addiction. It's the last article, but it's linked to the first one. A huge drug cartel network that produces and distributes drugs all over the world. Profiteering, speculation, profit. This network was created and continues to grow simply for the sake of profit. Physical money can be taken, hidden, stored, laundered and changed into commodities and baby. But no one will be able to change or hide our numbers. So the question is very simple. What kind of payment would a drug dealer actually accept from a buyer if there is no physical money? Milk? Bacon? Diamond earrings? Not. Our system will control all pawn shops, organizations for the exchange of goods or the distribution of goods for the poor. So the dealer will have nothing to accept. It will not be possible for him to profit on the basis of unfair trading and settlement of some money, because there will be none. Nor precious metal and other materials for the purpose of exchange and monetization. There will be no money, so the merchant would not gain anything. Of course, he will have a microchip implanted in his left hand, so he could accept payment by numbers. But under what heading? Paying for drugs? Definitely not. And it will not be possible to fool this system or accept bank numbers and change them under another item to bypass the system. It will not be possible to collect anything that would bring profit to such an organization.

And so, dear ones, it is already clear what will happen. The NFO will never allow such an organized crime network to emerge. There will be no more drug cartel, no dealer... because the dealers will not have the opportunity to collect, earn and get rich. Today we have a new system and if we implement it soon, it will not allow such evil to occur at all.

Dear friends, by introducing the NFO, we can destroy the entire drug underworld, drug cartels, drug barons and their criminal collaborators, smuggling routes and the network of drug production laboratories. This can be done within 24 hours of our anti-drug system being in place. We will change the physical money, which until now the drug cartels have in the banks, to our numbers. We will check them and nationalize them for the company. We will virtually erase organized crime for profit from our subsequent history of human society. Future generations of people will learn about it only from history textbooks as a corrupt system of the old world, or from sites interested in history on the Internet. New possibilities are opening up for us, how to create and prepare a new world of security for citizens and company. This time, we will no longer shift the possibilities and means of generating profit into the hands of citizens. We will create a secure system and within it we will own all organizations and assets. The citizen will get everything he needs and even more. We take care of everyone. There will be no more homeless or bankrupt. Firms, enterprises, banks and various other companies will remain only in our hands. We will manage everything so that the citizen does not have to worry about the leadership and running of the state, but only about himself and his family. We will take responsibility for the entire system and its operation. Every person will get the opportunity to work where he likes. We will also introduce a new benefit system for society. Some form of charity in which disadvantaged or disabled citizens will be able to work. No dictatorship, no oppression and persecution of citizens. We will find a life path for everyone as much as possible. And thus every single person will be a benefit to society. We have already learned from the history of our society that dictatorship and oppression lead nowhere. Eventually they fail, the system collapses and they are left with nothing but suffering and bad memories. That is why we brought together political scientists, statisticians, psychologists, economists and other experts. We have created a new system for society, from which we have eliminated all the errors of previous centuries of chaos.

It is clear to us that even in the new system some ailments will appear among the citizens. But we will try to eliminate them in the bud. We will put the financial system into operation and our observers (psychologists, mathematicians, statisticians, economists, philosophers, scientists and political scientists) will follow the development of this system. With the help of experts, we will correct the directions of development that will be shown to us and which we will follow. And if we see that some dangerous social phenomenon threatening citizens is beginning to emerge, we will intervene immediately.

At this first meeting, we focused on clarifying the principles of NFO and explaining how quickly we deal with adverse phenomena in society. In the next part of our first meeting, we have chipping on the agenda.

So for now I have roughly explained the principle of introducing bank numbers and abolishing physical money. Of course, everything cannot be explained during one meeting. This is just an introduction for you to understand what we are planning and preparing for the new society and the new world. The New World Order cannot be applied and implemented without this financial order. As long as physical money exists, we will not move anywhere. So it will happen that we will continue to fumble for the next centuries, problems in society will increase, including crime, and we will find ourselves in other wars. And I don't see any other real options that could be used in society to improve the lives of millions of people.

I can't wait until after the lunch break and I'll get to the second part of this meeting - chipping.

Dear, can you please go to our dining room? You have an hour to relax and have a coffee. We will meet in this secret room at exactly 1 pm. I am looking forward to the next lecture.

# Second point. Chipping of citizens.

Ladies and gentlemen, I welcome you to the second part of this meeting. I will focus on the part focused on the chipping of citizens and the chips themselves. At the outset, I would like to point out something else about the first part of Fr crime, so that we can smoothly follow up on the next topic. The third type of crime, which includes crimes of hatred, passion, greed, or crimes related to the morbid tendencies of some people are difficult to eliminate. These crimes are as old as humanity itself. I do not believe that we will be able to remove these ills from society. Well, our defense and law enforcement agencies will monitor and intervene also in the case of these types of crime. Here, however, the NFO will not have the opportunity to reach the very heart, the soul of a person, and therefore we must get to the very essence of this problem. It is about a person and people, about their relationships. Unfortunately, even unhappy, unrequited love is the cause of crime. We are only human. We will try to lead our company to friendship and good coexistence. We will already teach in primary schools how men should respect women. And vice versa. We will develop activities aimed at families, at their good coexistence, at their maintenance. We would like the enormous disintegration of families not to occur as it is today. All this, which I have just mentioned, we will discuss at our second meeting next time. It will concern the organization of society and various social aspects, the form of states and the entire civilized world. But today we will stick to the pre-agreed specific points of the meeting.

So, dear ones, what is population chipping and the chips themselves? We live in an era of rapidly developing technology in many areas of the production sphere, but the most interesting for us at the moment, because it concerns chips, is the global computer network. It also gives us many opportunities to fight crime. In addition to it, we have available new technical equipment and new investigative possibilities. They will help us in the investigation of violent crimes, kidnappings and other terrible acts that make life miserable in society.

Now I will tell you briefly what the electronic chip in the left hand of the citizen will be able to do.

So nice and tidy.

Our biotronics has already advanced to such a stage that we already have these chips ready and are even testing them on volunteers. Of course, a chip is an electronic thing. But it is modified and disinfected in such a way that we put it in a special biotronic plastic, which does not harm human health at all. It has no impact on life and does not cause allergies. It can be said that after applying it on the left wrist of a citizen, it is the same as if we did not apply anything there. On the health side.

What can this chip do?!

It monitors the health status of the citizen. In case of sudden deterioration, such as collapses, seizures or other failure of an organ of the human body, it is able to immediately send a signal to the nearest medical center, thereby summoning help and saving the patient's life.

It works like an ATM card without a card. It is directly connected and registered in the main banking center. It can be used to pay and receive payments. Carry out all possible bank transactions.

It has localization ability. It can find a citizen even in the most remote places on Earth. It even sends a signal from underground. It will ensure perfect control over the safety of the citizen throughout his life (we are already at the end of the production of a special localization chip for children). I will explain that later.

And last but not least, it contains the identification data of the citizen, for example, such as an ID card, a health card, etc many other documents hidden in the personal information database related to the needs of each individual.

It is clear that over time these chips will be able to perform many more tasks and provide many conveniences. A completely new system of society is opening before us, with endless innovations and possibilities that even we cannot imagine at the moment. Now we stand at the very beginning.

I will come back to the two parts. I will give you an example: Citizen X goes somewhere from home and does not return home on the same day. He will never come back. No one knows what happened and where he disappeared to. There is no way to locate and save him. The police will declare a search and use their methods and everything available at their disposal. But this citizen is still missing and the search leads nowhere (except for solved cases and found persons, of course). A few years have passed since the day of his disappearance, and no one hopes to find him. And so this citizen X disappeared forever.

In the new social system, the chip will also be in contact with the localization center ensuring security, but after the decision a voluntary registration of an adult citizen. IN the new world will not be able to use any directive or violent methods. Everyone will be able to choose where and how they can register, and thus be under more or less control. So I'll cut it short. If citizen X from the old world had an electronic chip in his left hand and was locatable, our security system would locate him by coordinates and send a special security force after him to find him very quickly. She would save his life. K such things can also happen spontaneously without any intention. A citizen can get lost somewhere in in the mountains, in the forests... After declaring a search by the family or someone else, the system immediately locates him and the rescue team will try to get him to safety as soon as possible.

We will establish a special law for the protection of the youngest children. We will chip them after they turn three years old. Children tend to get lost most often through no fault of their own. We must create a system for the special protection of children. We must no longer allow the possibility of their loss or abduction. No way. We will bring the system to such perfection that children will be protected in the new world as they have never been before. We will guide them to acquire important knowledge and thus become the most important pillar of the new order. We will eradicate from society the insane attempts to harm others or terrorize others, but also the perversions that society has to deal with on a daily basis. In the new social order, the family will come first. And that in a defined relationship - a man and a woman. We will not tolerate any other madness that is contrary to what we came into the world with. This old world has become very sick and cannot be cured. The cup of bitterness was filled to the brim. That's why we send the old system to the lost. We will establish a new order - NFO. And on new pillars we will build a new world that will shape a new person. A person who will love nature and the world around him. But we will discuss that next time at the second meeting. Today's rally has its own goal. After the meeting, you will receive a manual that you must study. It has exactly 500 pages. You don't have to remember everything you read in it. Each of you will familiarize yourself with the text of one chapter in detail. We have selected tasks tailored for each of you. We know your psychological profile and your abilities. We know that you can easily do it and you will be successful. If you study and understand the chapter assigned to you, it will be necessary for you to dispose of the manual. They burned. It must not fall into other unauthorized hands, as you have been instructed. Your tasks will be clearly and simply explained.

This new order of the social world will stand on ten pillars. You are sitting here exactly ten. Each of you will have to guide the building of one of the pillars. We put our hope in you and you have our absolute trust. You have sworn loyalty.

So, dear ones, each of you received one manual on the table. The instructions are clear. We are coming to the end of this first meeting. Where will the second rally be held? You will find out later, but the time of the next meeting has not been determined. It is not scheduled yet. However, it will be held in a different place than here. You will receive a message from our messengers.

Dear friends, this is the beginning of a new world that we will build on the basis of the new NFO financial order. The entire new social system will have ten pillars. Ten messengers a ten commissioners. I'm the eleventh. After the second meeting, my task will be over. You will never hear from me or see me again.

It's high time to get started. You will all know what to do and where to turn. We never send each other written messages or links in any other way. We only receive them verbally and personally from our messengers. No one has the ability to intercept our communications. We are here to resurrect a new better society. This old one is already failing. Man does not respect man. Love, feelings, family... no longer play a big role for many people in this world. Perversions are promoted and sick-minded examples are presented even to young citizens. And what is the worst? Even for children in kindergartens. Where would it all go if we didn't try to intervene? To social catastrophe and to the disintegration of modern society.

The nations of the world still haven't learned from the disasters that happened to people in the past. For example, what was the destruction of the cities of Sodom and Gomorrah. And we don't want to allow that anymore! Get to work! This time we will build a new system that will not be disturbed or questioned.

The citizen is everything to us. Family is everything to us. The health of citizens and the planet come first. Protection of life and citizens are the most important. Welcome to the new world we are about to build!

Physical money, currency and other securities... we will send directly to hell! Because that's where they came from.

Abolition of physical money - it will not be possible without chipping citizens. As man and woman. One cannot exist without the other.

Look in the world for what unites us. Well, how to do it in in this world where there are still some supreme principles of division?

End of the first meeting.

www.ingramcontent.com/pod-product-compliance
Lightning Source LLC
LaVergne TN
LVHW041444170726
843492LV00008B/2808